More Books by Amy Perez MS Psychology:

- <u>Psychological Thriller Stories</u>
- <u>The Plunge: All about Love and Relationships</u>
- <u>Manic Episode Series</u>
- <u>3rd Times a Charm</u>
- <u>The Dark Angel Episode Series</u>
- <u>Bipolar Disorder: Thriving Triggers, Love & Relationships</u>
- <u>Bipolar Disorder: Triggers, Boundaries and Roadblocks</u>
- <u>Bipolar Disorder: Love and Relationships</u>
- <u>Bipolar Disorder: Pregnancy & Childbirth</u>
- <u>Bipolar Disorder: Substances, Sex and Major Life Changes</u>

- *21 Keys Episode Series*
- *The Anxiety Warriors*
- *Schizophrenic Episode Series*
- *The Psychology of Love, Finances, and Nutrition*
- *Narcissistic Episode Series*
- *10 Ways to Thrive with Bipolar Disorder*

10 Ways to Thrive
With Bipolar Disorder

Amy Perez

MS

Psychology

Table of Contents

Introduction 1

Money 6

Nutrition 13

Fitness 23

Self Care 29

Sleep and Relaxation 37

Triggers 44

Boundaries 51

Education 57

Medication 61

Working 68

Bipolar Disorder: Triggers Boundaries and Roadblocks(Preview) 76

Published in 2018

Copyright 2018

ISBN: 978-1983265747

Printed by Amazon

All rights reserved. No part of this publication may be reproduced, distributed or transmitted in any form or by any means, including photocopying, recording, or other electronic or mechanical methods, without prior written permission of the publisher except in the case of brief quotations embodied in critical reviews and certain noncommercial uses permitted by copyright law. For permission requests, write to the publisher, addressed "Attention: Permissions" at the address below.

Front Cover Design by Author.

Book Design by Designer.

Author: Amy Perez MS Psychology

Visit Amy Perez MS Psychology's Author Page!

10 Ways to Thrive With Bipolar Disorder

Introduction

Bipolar disorder is not the end of the world. There I said it. It is not who you are. It is part of who you are. We are no different than someone with high blood pressure or diabetes. In the same way a person with diabetes would check their blood sugar, eat healthy and exercise, those of us with bipolar disorder can keep up a healthy mental and physical lifestyle. It is highly possible to live a happy, productive life while also having bipolar disorder.

The reason I know this is because I lead one. I am a wife and a mother. I own a pet and take care of a household. I have a Bachelor's degree and a Master's degree. I have worked with underprivileged people living with various mental health issues. Lastly, I am an author of various mental health books. Do I have lows? Yes. Do I have highs? Absolutely. But just like checking my blood sugar, I check in with my moods throughout the day. Bipolar disorder is a mood disorder after all.

Am I feeling low? Why? Am I too energetic for no reason? It does take work but it can be manageable. I have an arsenal of tools from nutritional factors to psychological factors. I also have certain family and friends to rely on in a time of need or crisis. Also, I keep a close working relationship with my doctor. This book breaks down the ten areas of anyone's life that are very important. But especially for us with bipolar disorder, it is important for us to keep track of our bodies and minds.

For anyone fresh out of the hospital or newly diagnosed, just take it slow. There is a lot to digest. And remember, I've been there. I was Baker Acted three times. Baker Acted, for those who do not know is basically when you are held by law in a mental hospital. It is scary and taxing on your brain. I have tried and failed many times with medication. I have gone off of my meds thinking that I didn't need them. I have been suicidal. I have battled with self-medication with drugs and alcohol. I have sabotaged relationships from bipolar disorder rages. I have made poor sexual and financial decisions from hypomania, mania and depression. Does any of that sound familiar?

If so, you are in the right place. If you are a loved one of someone with bipolar disorder, guess what? So am I. So, it looks like we have a few things in common. My Master's degree is in Psychology and my Bachelor's degree is in Nutrition. I was diagnosed with bipolar disorder in 2010. I have been hospital free for over six years. I have lived with bipolar disorder in my family since birth.

Amy Perez MS Psychology

The encouraging news is that those of us with bipolar disorder can live well and be in society as productive members. We don't have to hide ourselves. It is okay to have a mental illness. I see my psychiatrist regularly and I take my medication daily. My loved ones and close friends are all aware of my illness. I openly talk about how I am feeling. I share my feelings and the people close to me share theirs too. I am happy to share with you as well!

Those of us with bipolar disorder can embrace our diagnosis and help support each other. We are all in this together. Life can be difficult. Just managing basic tasks like showering and cooking can feel like climbing a mountain. But we can thrive just as much as anyone else can. These ten areas of my life are very important. Each one of them can be problematic for those of us with bipolar disorder. And that's okay. We are learning and growing every day!

Money

You may be curious why I decided to start with money. Well, we all need money to survive. We have to buy food, pay bills, buy clothing and entertainment. For some of us, not all of our medication is covered by insurance. Therefore, money becomes especially important for someone with bipolar disorder. It is very easy to get caught up in hypomania or just extra excitement and overspend. It can be hard to stick to a budget or even make a budget.

Two years ago, I went to pick up my medicine from the pharmacy expecting to pay no more than fifteen dollars. My total for my medication that I needed was three hundred dollars. There was a gap in my insurance and I wasn't covered for the full amount. I found myself at the mercy of family to get the medication I needed. I didn't have an emergency fund set up. I was not prepared for an extra expense.

On the extreme end, credit cards in the middle of a mall can be catastrophic. For me, the holidays can trigger me and I will overspend. Those of us with bipolar disorder can get into serious debt with credit cards. For me, excessive shopping and financial hiccups can be a sign that I'm feeling manic. This can be a queue for me to open up to my husband and tell him how I'm feeling. A doctor appointment may be necessary.

However, I do pay my own bills and manage savings accounts. I do have credit cards but my husband keeps them hidden. Anyone can battle with credit cards. I know that I will be triggered in a mall or with online shopping with my credit cards. I was open and honest about this problem area and now it is managed.

Amy Perez MS Psychology

The lesson there is just being honest with yourself and others about how bipolar disorder can have a negative impact on finances. At the moment, I have cut up all of my credit cards except for two. It is good to find someone you can trust to at least be aware of your spending and to help give you advice. If you find that this problem area is over your head, make sure you speak to a doctor or counselor. Impulse control can be an issue and gambling could also be an issue. There are gambling hotlines in different states and cities that can help with that separately.

There are ways that those of us with bipolar disorder can handle money on our own. I have seen loved ones struggle in this area. Also, in my online groups, this area can cause problems. Some people seem to have simply given up. There are ways to set up your accounts to be successful. Here is an example:

Checking: $500.00

Savings: $200.00

Emergency Fund: $300.00

Fun/Vacations: $120.00

Gifts: $75.00

Kids: $100.00

Roth IRA: $75.00

My money is broken down into categories. My basic needs such as medication, food, gas and beauty supplies come from my checking account. My savings account is set up for little things that come up. I may need to pay a little extra for medicine or have an unexpected car repair. I have myself covered for unexpected expenses. Every time I earn money whether it is a paycheck or a gift, I will split off about twenty percent in this account. Another ten percent will go into the rest of the accounts. If a holiday or birthday is coming up, I may add more money into my gift account.

The emergency fund is set up for job loss or something out of my control. The fun and vacations account are set up for a weekend treat like a carnival or maybe a manicure. The gift account is set up for when my loved ones and friends have birthdays and for Christmas. This account keeps me from overspending on gifts which is my trouble area. The account for my kids is set up for when they want to join a sport or take lessons. Also, if anyone goes through a growth spurt, I'm covered.

Finally, my Roth IRA is set up for my future. There can also be separate accounts for stocks and CDs as well. Many bank accounts allow up to six free accounts. If overspending is an issue, alerts can be set up through the bank account. If accounts go below a certain amount, alerts can be emailed to you or a designated person.

A more extreme measure to take, if this area is largely problematic is to keep larger sums of money in an account that doesn't have a debit card attached to it. A second person required to withdraw money can also be a good measure.

Typically, financial mistakes can be repaired. I found it to be helpful to just focus on the future instead of dwelling on the past when it comes to finances. There are many finance books available for free at local libraries.

Amy Perez MS Psychology

Nutrition

This is one of my favorite subjects to talk about. Many of us with bipolar disorder can suffer weight gain from medication, bouts of depression or both. Until I got a reduction in medication, I was suffering from extreme food cravings. I literally could not stop eating fried food, chocolate and candy. I packed on thirty pounds in less than a year. It is possible to maintain a healthy weight and take medication. It does take some work and dedication.

I like to watch nutrition videos online, read health magazines and read nutrition books. Nutrition is a science and it is always changing. What we eat can have an impact on our moods and some foods can even have a bad reaction to our medicine. For instance, for one of my pills, I cannot eat grapefruit or drink grapefruit juice. Isn't that interesting?

One area for those of us with bipolar disorder that can make nutrition difficult is impulse control. Anyone can see a commercial for a pizza and be driven to order some. Not all people with bipolar disorder will battle with impulse control but some people might. Depression could make it worse. On the flip side, during hypo mania or mania, appetite can be severely reduced or non-existent.

Depression can be a time when certain foods are appealing. For instance, cocoa can naturally uplift our mood. It is no wonder that sweets with chocolate can make us feel better. Food is a wonderful thing for anyone. We celebrate with loved ones with food, we go out to eat and eat for entertainment. Also, alcohol can be involved during these occasions.

This is worth mentioning because those of us with bipolar disorder don't need to suffer with alcoholism on top of our illness. If you feel this area is a problem for you, absolutely seek help. Alcohol may trigger bipolar disorder symptoms and react negatively with our medication. Make sure to ask your doctor if you are able to drink on your medication. I myself decided to heavily limit myself when it comes to alcohol. For me, it just isn't worth it. Alcohol is a depressant. The morning after having more than one drink, I will find myself feeling down.

With alcohol, I have found that my true loved ones and friends accept me for who I am. They are comfortable with the fact that I don't drink very much. If someone makes you feel like you need to drink to be in their life, maybe rethink the relationship with them. That would be a great place to set some boundaries which we will discuss later.

If I want to wind down with a drink at the end of the night, I will make an iced chamomile tea. Chamomile relaxes the body and mind naturally. When thinking about drinking alcohol to bring down manic symptoms, think about talking to your doctor first. Ask if it is okay to take melatonin supplements or they may prescribe you something different. Melatonin can be bought over the counter.

Another chemical of choice by many of us is caffeine. I love coffee. Coffee keeps me going especially as a parent and as an author. Sometimes I plan on sleeping until eight o'clock but wake up at five. So, yes caffeine plays a role in my life. However, too much caffeine can be bad for anyone. Caffeine can have an effect on the mood. The fact that bipolar disorder is a mood disorder makes this area important. Be careful with caffeine. Talk to your doctor about a safe amount for you.

10 Ways to Thrive With Bipolar Disorder

    I personally know how some medicine can make us tired and out of it. I make sure to rotate coffee with tea, juice and almond milk. Also, caffeine too late in the day can make it hard to sleep at night. Also, worth mentioning, a lot of caffeinated drinks contain a lot of sugar which can lead to weight gain. It seems like sugar is hidden everywhere. Make sure to read labels and keep track of sugar intake. Women can have twenty-five grams of sugar a day and men can have thirty-seven.

    It is important for us with bipolar disorder to eat! We should eat whole foods and enjoy food. Cooking and learning new recipes can make us feel better. However, when we are feeling down or low on energy, it's a great idea to keep healthy and easy meals on hand. Also, have restaurants in mind that offer healthy options for when cooking isn't an option. Increasingly, there are more restaurants and grocery stores offering delivery options. These are great for planning ahead or last-minute meals.

Keeping fresh snacks like nuts, apples and bananas is a good idea too. I keep nuts and fruit in my purse and car at all times. It helps with stress from traffic and I find myself staying away from fast food more. These foods are good for us, help with mood and maintain a healthy weight. Keeping a schedule for eating is good too. Make sure to eat breakfast, lunch and dinner. Add two or three snacks in between. I make sure to eat a healthy snack when I take my medicine. I will do a yogurt and banana at night. Sometimes, medicine can upset our stomachs if we don't eat enough or eat the wrong thing. Make sure to check with your doctor about any foods that can react with your medicine.

Most importantly, enjoy food that you love! Two or three times a week, make sure to treat yourself with a favorite meal or snack. Go out with friends or loved ones and enjoy food. It is important for our mood to have a healthy relationship with food. Stay away from fad diets and don't limit your calories too much. We need our brains and bodies working at an optimal level. Starving ourselves is not the answer. Also, weight loss pills and supplements can have a bad reaction for us. Some of them contain high levels of caffeine or other harmful chemicals. It is important that we treat our bodies well because it impacts our brain and vice versa.

Here is an example of a typical daily meal plan with a medication schedule:

9:30 a.m. Breakfast

1 hard-boiled egg

1 cup of oatmeal

1 banana

Amy Perez MS Psychology

1 glass of orange juice

1 cup of coffee

11:00 a.m. Snack

½ cup of almonds

1 apple

12:30 p.m. Lunch

1 black bean or chicken taco

1 side salad

1 cup of low-fat milk or almond milk

1 cookie

(Medicine)

3:30 p.m. Snack

Tea, coffee or juice

1 protein bar or oatmeal

6:00 p.m. Dinner

6 ounces of salmon

1 cup of broccoli

1 cup of mashed potatoes

9:30 p.m. Snack

Choose 2 or 3:

- Yogurt
- Berries
- Granola
- Popcorn
- Cheese
- Banana

(Medicine)

At night, I will have a snack with my medicine and read a book or listen to music.

Sometimes, those of us with bipolar disorder have trouble falling asleep at night. We will talk about that soon.

On the weekend or on a date night, I will enjoy fried food or pizza. I get treats with the kids on occasion also. Nutrition does coincide with fitness which we will discuss next.

Fitness

This area can be very difficult for those of us with bipolar disorder. Sometimes just getting out of bed is a challenge. Practicing self-care does come before fitness for me but I feel that they can go hand in hand. Bipolar disorder symptoms can make showering and grooming seem like mountains to climb. Sometimes depression gets ahold of us and we just have a deep need to lie down and maybe even sleep. But if we can overcome this, we can win. By all means, if you need to lie down because your mind is overworked or you are feeling overwhelmed then definitely do so. But just don't stay there.

Most importantly, speak to your doctor before starting an exercise program. With exercise, our body can feel more energetic. Also, exercise can help clear the mind. Fitness does not have to be constant. Just setting a small goal can be life changing and lifesaving. Fitness is especially important for those of us with bipolar disorder. It is important to try and be the best version of ourselves.

The best version could be a five-minute walk or a thirty-minute swim. We may not always have something to give. But when we do, let's do it! When we exercise, we are giving a gift to ourselves. The idea is to fight the feeling. Do the opposite of what we feel. For example, when I get the sudden urge to lie down and give up, I do exactly that. I give into myself; I lie down. However, I set an alarm on my phone for thirty minutes. I let myself feel my feelings. Whether it's anxiety, depression or maybe even regret.

I curl up in a ball and deal with the feelings. Next, I picture myself ridding my body and mind of the emotions. I could walk to a local store, go swimming or on a bike ride with the family. The physical activity to come can fight the negative feelings. Workout videos are available online for free or joining a gym is great if it's in the budget. The gym can be a great place for someone with bipolar disorder. It's just as good for us as it is for someone with high blood pressure or diabetes.

But what if you just can't? Your brain is fighting you. Getting up and moving around is becoming an issue. This is when we get help. There are counseling services available. Many gyms offer trainers. Keep your doctor in the loop. Depression could be taking over. Make sure to talk to a psychiatrist, psychologist or general physician for help. We owe it to ourselves to stay active. It activates the feel-good hormones that will benefit someone with bipolar disorder.

No one can force you to do it. There are ways that I stay motivated to stay fit. I find just surrounding

Amy Perez MS Psychology

myself with positivity helps. I subscribe to fitness magazines and read online articles. Reading fitness journeys of others can motivate us. I found positivity in sharing my weight loss and activity with friends and family in person and on social media. Wearing a fitness bracelet can be motivating. Also, there are fitness apps.

After my son was born, I had gained over fifty pounds. I had a lot of weight that I wanted to lose. There were days that I didn't even want to get out of bed. It just so happens that those are the days that I did my best. I would wake up and just take it step by step. I would just tell myself that I was going to walk for ten minutes on the treadmill. Some days it would take me two hours just to get ready and go. Of course, the negative thoughts would rush in. My brain told me there was no point or I wouldn't lose the weight.

But I had to fight back. I would stretch my workout pants over my thighs and trudge to the gym. I went from a size sixteen to a size six. When I couldn't run, I walked. When I couldn't walk, I swam. I gave myself as much as I could. Once I would start walking, I would say why not jog for ten seconds? After ten seconds, I realized I could push a little more. Sometimes I hated it. It was difficult. I felt big and uncomfortable. I was fighting my brain and my body.

Once I worked fitness into my schedule, it helped me maintain a stable day and week. It gave me a structure all week long.

Here is a sample week of fitness:

Monday: Off Day Practice Self Care and Relax

Tuesday: Run 1 Mile

Wednesday: Weight Train

Amy Perez MS Psychology

Thursday: Day Off Self Care

Friday: Swim 30 Minutes

Saturday: Run 1 Mile

Sunday: Off Day Do Chores and Grocery Shop

However, I did like how it would lift my mood. Now running is a hobby and I added more fun workouts to it. My husband and kids join me now on a regular basis. Fitness is now part of my self-care. Self-care is very important and we will talk about that next.

Self Care

When someone has any medical condition, it is of utmost importance to put themselves and their health first. Even if someone is in picture perfect health, self-care is so important. When we take good care of ourselves, we feel better. Period. This means we work on ourselves with time, energy and money. Scheduling proper time for showering, grooming and for women, makeup and hair should be included. Using a schedule can keep us on track with self-care. For example, every day from nine o'clock to eleven o'clock is time to get ready.

Does everyone need this amount of time to get ready? Maybe not. But someone with bipolar disorder may need extra time. What if I start feeling depressed while I'm getting out of the shower? What if I need to lie down for a few minutes? This happens. Let it happen in stages. Just get through the shower and put on basic clothing. Then see how you feel. Maybe stop for a snack or tea. If you feel better then work on hair or makeup.

It doesn't always have to be one hundred percent. Of course, I want to shower, blow-dry my hair, put make-up on and dress up. Many days my brain and body won't let me. This is where the self-pep talk comes in. I just tell myself that I will take a quick shower and that's it. Surprisingly, once I'm in the shower, I will feel the motivation to wash my hair and shave. Many times, after a shower, I just need to lie down for a few minutes.

But guess what? I got that shower in. Getting clean can often times be a challenge for us with bipolar disorder. Many times, when I chat with my peers with bipolar disorder, I see that this is a challenge. Add to that the fact that many of us have pets, kids and/or other people to take care of, this can be a mountain to climb for sure!

We just need to understand that we need to put ourselves first. It isn't selfish, it's just necessary. Another issue that can come up is dental hygiene. Sometimes, by the end of the night, self-care can feel like swimming across an ocean. Feeling tired mixed with depressive or manic symptoms can make it difficult to wash up for bed or brush my teeth. The important thing is to practice self-care when we are feeling good.

For instance, I am feeling great after dinner. Many times, I take this opportunity to brush and floss my teeth and use mouthwash. This may seem strange to some people. But if I have a banana and yogurt with my medicine at nine at night and maybe fall asleep, I already cleaned my teeth really good earlier in the evening. Some dentists suggest brushing our teeth three times a day. So, brushing a third time at night is fine.

Always remember, you cannot pour from an empty cup. If our health fails, we cannot give to others. If we need to put the phone away and take a nap, that's okay. If we are feeling great at three in the afternoon and have energy to take a shower, that's great! When we are feeling on the up side, that is the time to focus on ourselves and our wellness.

Anyone with bipolar disorder knows that when we are feeling great, it doesn't always last a long time. If we are feeling great and then we get triggered, our mood can change. If our mood changes too much, we might lose our motivation for self-care. We will go deep into what triggers are and how to deal with them later in the book. It is important to know that for us with bipolar disorder, self-care can take an entire day or the over the course of a few days. Just showering and combing our hair can take a couple of hours.

That is okay. It is completely normal. Some of us have bipolar disorder with other mental illnesses such as anxiety or a personality disorder. Others battle with addiction. That is okay. Working with our illness alongside other challenges is what makes our day unique. But if we start with our shower and get dried off, that sense of accomplishment can motivate us to do more. Just make getting clean a priority.

Even if we get hospitalized, having a habit of getting clean can help us get better faster. Having that routine can get our brain back to being stable faster. I know this because I went through it. When I was hospitalized the first and second time, I barely practiced self-care. It took me months to get better. The third time I was hospitalized it was different. Even though I was manic, I requested a shower and a toothbrush. I used the lotion they provided. I used the little comb they gave us. That was my final time being hospitalized.

Since then, I have made myself care a priority. Often times, I will go to the gym just to get in a shower. The whole process could take two hours and that's okay. People who live free of mental illness may not understand this just like how we may not understand the self-care needs of others. Someone who is an amputee or someone with cancer will have their own self care needs that I don't understand. And that's okay. That is why education is so important. We will talk more about education in a later chapter.

One important thing to mention is self-care and medication. Some of our medication can make us tired. Never shower or bath after taking medicine that makes you tired and sleepy. I lost two family members because they mixed their psychiatric drugs with alcohol and were in water. If you need to be monitored during self-care that is okay. Make sure that you let your loved ones know. There is no shame, I've been there.

    Also, if you are triggered by self-care items like razors or nail files, tell someone immediately. That is one thing I take very seriously. There is nothing wrong with going to the doctor or emergency room with problems that are bigger than us. People are there to help people like us. It's just the same as having a fever or severe stomach pain. It's an emergency. There could be something chemically wrong in the brain that can be solved with medications. Just as important as self-care is getting enough sleep and being able to relax. These two are important for everyone, especially us.

Amy Perez MS Psychology

Sleep and Relaxation

Last year I went into a doctor's office for a vein treatment in my legs. Part of my self-care after the procedure was to put my feet up. I just so happen to have a seat that reclines so that's what I did. When dinner was in the oven, I put my feet up. Before bed, I would put my feet up. I would follow the daily routine and relax. It felt very weird at first. I remember making excuses. I would reiterate that my doctor told me to put my feet up. Why did I feel embarrassed to relax?

It was almost unnatural. That is when I realized how important it is to relax. Relaxation was so foreign to me. I was either lying in bed sleeping or working like a busy bee. There was no in between. I have come to realize that my bipolar brain works that way if I'm un-medicated. My brain and body could be completely down or going a mile a minute. Therefore, finding the in between was a challenge. I did it by force. But how? How do you find an in between?

I wanted to be awake and alert yet relaxed. I wanted to just hang out and be present. It takes time and practice. One thing I find hard is fighting the urge to isolate when I need to relax. So, when I get the urge to do so, I find a relaxing hobby to do. I now have a long list of relaxing activities to choose from. Here is a list of relaxing activities I draw from when I'm feeling high or low:

- Write
- Read
- Color
- Paint
- Have a healthy snack
- Sip tea or coffee
- Listen to music

- Watch a show
- Paint nails
- Online shop
- Check finances and make goals
- Make weekend plans
- Write in a journal
- Look up new recipes
- Make a to do list
- Call or text a friend
- Plan gifts for holidays
- Make a budget
- Research topics online
- Read about health
- Read blogs

These are just some of the things we can do during relaxation. I force myself to relax physically and work on things that will improve my life. I am present with my family or friends and engaged. Some of these can be done together. I can make a snack and write while relaxing. I can put music on and paint. The painting could then become a gift for someone. Products can come from our relaxation.

It may seem lazy or selfish at first. But our bipolar disorder deserves the same treatment as a physical ailment or physical recovery. Many times, bipolar disorder can feel more physical than anything. There are physical activities that can also be relaxing. Going for a light swim can help people relax. Some people enjoy yoga classes as well. There are many yoga videos online as well. An hour should be our minimum of relaxation per day. Some of us may need more than that. That is okay and it's normal.

In addition to the important relaxation is sleep. Everyone needs a certain amount of sleep per night. Anyone that is on medication may need more sleep than someone who is not. Getting on a regular sleep schedule is important for those of us with bipolar disorder. With my medication, I need nine hours of sleep per night. If I don't get enough sleep during the night, I make sure to schedule a nap during the day. We all know how we feel when we do not get enough sleep.

Sleep is important to keep us stable. Not sleeping enough or sleeping too much can be warning signs. Make sure to talk with your doctor or therapist if you are having trouble sleeping or can't get out of bed. Sometimes I will drink tea with chamomile to get tired. Also, melatonin will do the trick for me. Some people who have anxiety on top of bipolar disorder might need different treatments to fall asleep. I have additional medication that I can take if my anxiety spikes while I am trying to sleep.

Staying active during the day can also get us tired for good sleep at night. Shutting off technology an hour or two before bed can help for sleep as well. Also, avoiding triggers before bed is important. If anyone in your life tends to trigger your symptoms, do not message them close to bedtime. Getting on a nighttime routine is important especially if medication is taken nightly. Read for an hour while having a light snack or listen to music and draw. Escaping into a hobby for us can be therapeutic.

Before I get too tired, I take my medicine and brush my teeth. If I have trouble sleeping, I will try for thirty minutes to fall asleep on my own. I first make sure that it isn't the temperature in the room or uncomfortable clothing that is making it hard to sleep. If the thirty minutes goes by and I can't sleep, I consider chamomile tea or melatonin. Make sure to discuss with your doctor if you want to try melatonin for sleep, it may not be for everyone. He or she will know a safe bedtime regimen for you.

Lastly, if necessary, medicine that is taken as needed may be used. I always make sure that my closest family and my doctor are aware if I am having trouble sleeping. For me, this could be a sign of hypomania or mania coming on. Conversely, if I am having trouble getting out of bed and having negative feelings, it can be a warning sign of depression. Depression can show up in the sleep schedule. Sleep and relaxation are two important areas for those of us with bipolar disorder.

Amy Perez MS Psychology

Triggers

There has been a lot of attention on the news and in social media revolving around triggers and trigger warnings. So much so, that some people have even made jokes about triggers. But triggers are nothing to joke around about. Even if we are diligent in taking our medicine, seeing our doctor, and administering self-care, triggers can show up and make our bipolar symptoms show.

The first time I heard of a trigger was fourteen years ago. I was working in a steakhouse. I was told that nonalcoholic frozen drinks must come in a normal shaped cup. If a frozen nonalcoholic drink was put in a bar glass, it could trigger a recovering alcoholic to want an alcoholic drink. I didn't question it. I just rolled with it. If only everyone could just recognize common triggers and move on. However, it's not that simple. For instance, I love to hear children laughing and playing. I find joy in watching little people have fun. My house is many times loud with screaming and laughing children. I am used to it. Other people come over and are surprised at the screams.

I can tell that visitors are uneasy with the children running around and screaming. My sweet, lovely children and their friends trigger negative feelings in my loved ones and friends. Does this mean that they don't love me and my children? Absolutely not. It's just that they are not used to the commotion that my children make and it might be triggering stress, anxiety and/or bipolar symptoms. Like I said in the beginning of the book, I am a family member of people with bipolar disorder. Interestingly enough, my friends and loved ones who do not have bipolar disorder seem to also be triggered by the different noises of children just as much if not more.

Amy Perez MS Psychology

Therefore, I try to take note of who can handle my children in certain ways and who cannot. When I am with one person, I might put on a movie for everyone to relax. With another person, I might grab a ball and head outside with everyone. It just depends on what each person can handle. If someone doesn't stay long, I completely understand. They may need to go home and relax. Maybe they need to take some medicine. I am happy to see my loved ones and friends taking care of themselves while still making time for me and my family.

Here is a list of the many triggers. Make sure to write some of your own and plan on working around them or maybe even avoid them all together:

- Alcohol
- Smoking
- Loud music
- Screaming babies or children

- Bright lights
- Heavy traffic
- Too many people talking at once
- Heat
- Cold
- Dim light
- Dirty environment
- Rude people
- Judgmental people
- Loud parties
- Big crowds
- Loneliness
- Lack of sleep
- Large workload
- Caffeine
- Sharp objects
- Fried food
- Spicy food

- Feeling unsafe
- Being around toxic people
- Abuse
- Stress
- Job loss
- Fighting
- Argumentative people
- School difficulty
- Basic life changes
- Hospitalization
- Family emergencies
- Traveling
- Financial problems

Any of these triggers can wreak havoc on anyone. Someone who is going through chemo or dialysis or even bloodwork could be triggered by any of these. Those of us with bipolar disorder are no different.

So, what happens when more than one trigger is happening at once? Say for instance, your top three triggers are financial stress, screaming children and extreme heat. Being trapped in a doctor's office that is hot with a child screaming while you are struggling to pay the bill will be very bad. Therefore, going to the doctor just to get needed medication can be a very stressful situation.

Discussing your triggers with loved ones can help them see life through your eyes. Write down your trigger and how it makes you feel. Here is an example:

Alcohol

When I am around alcohol, I feel that I may want to abuse it. I know that it doesn't mix well with my medication. Also, I am haunted by the memories of a drunk family member who died from an alcohol related incident.

I have recognized my trigger and wrote down how it makes me feel. Next, it is important for my family and friends to know how I feel. I still want to be included in their life, but I don't want to be pressured to drink alcohol. I let them know that if they drink it's fine. But if they want to hang out, we can go biking or swimming. We can drink tea or lemonade. That becomes my personal boundary which brings me to the next chapter.

10 Ways to Thrive With Bipolar Disorder

Amy Perez MS Psychology

Boundaries

Everyone everywhere has boundaries. However, I am always a little surprised when someone throws up a boundary at me. At first, I feel offended. I immediately go on the defensive. I can't believe that they are uncomfortable with something that I do or ask of them. The most recent boundary was set by a good friend of mine. She made me some soup but it was too spicy for me. I felt bad but I had to let her know. I mentioned that the next time, she could make it without spice for me. I even offered to pay for the ingredients. She seemed a little offended. But nonetheless, she took it with grace.

She also refused to make it without spice. She let me know that she would give me the recipe and I could make it myself. I immediately felt bad but I let it go. I ended up buying the ingredients and making it myself. It tasted amazing and my family loved it. She set a clear, firm boundary. She was not going to change her recipe for me. I kindly accepted her boundary and moved on. We are still the best of friends.

Her and I practice all sorts of boundaries together. We both have different lifestyles and life choices. Somehow, we find ways to balance our likes and dislikes and remain friends. But what if she didn't set that boundary? What if she had made me the soup without spice? She may have resented doing it.

If we never set boundaries with our loved ones and friends, they will never know that things make us uncomfortable. All of our triggers give us a right to make boundaries. As human beings, it is our right to set boundaries with people. For me, being married and having kids, making boundaries is a necessity in our household. Everyone needs to get clean, fed and enough sleep. Therefore, there are many boundaries that are set. We have boundaries in our house such as set eating times and sleep schedules.

Luckily, all of our friends, relatives and neighbors accept and respect them. If someone is abusing your boundaries, you have a right to let them know. I had a loved one who was not accepting my sleep schedule. My sleep schedule affects everyone around me. I spoke with this person about it. The person did change drastically. I earned their respect. Now, they call before they come over. They also do not call late at night or interrupt my sleep. Him and I remain very close. Our relationship has blossomed. Him and I have created many boundaries since then.

Had I just yelled at him and swore with anger, I may have severed the relationship. That was my fear. Boundaries are a great topic to share with close loved ones and friends. Also, therapists can help create them with you.

But what if the boundary has to be set within ourselves? What if our own behavior is wreaking havoc on our symptoms? It may seem strange, but I feel that I can be my own worst enemy. My boundary is work. If I do not set a boundary with myself, I will work around the clock. I won't eat, sleep or relax. Even self-care will suffer. Once I set a goal, I will work until I can't. This could be a blessing or a curse.

If I am working so hard that I can't sleep then that is very bad. I have set a work boundary with myself. When I am writing, I have to set a time frame otherwise I will write through my shower time. Also, I would just work and not make enough time for my family and friends.

Another example for me is more dietary, it's with caffeine. Caffeine seems to be everywhere. Personally, I love to drink coffee. However, I am already pretty energetic. If I drink too much caffeine, I could get too energetic and talkative. This could be bad for everyone around me. Many people in my life need me to be a listener more than a talker.

So, what happens if someone doesn't respect your boundaries or if you are having trouble with your own personal boundaries? I go more in depth when it comes to boundaries in *Bipolar Disorder: Triggers, Boundaries and Roadblocks*. This is where a health professional can be useful. Talking to a doctor or therapist can help. Even talking to friends and relatives can help. Journaling is useful too. I frequent the dollar store and craft stores for colorful notebooks and pens. Keep these handy for writing down troubles. Through writing, feelings can come out that we didn't know we had. In this way we our educating ourselves. We will talk about education next!

10 Ways to Thrive With Bipolar Disorder

Amy Perez MS Psychology

Education

If I could give myself some advice when I first got diagnosed, it would have been to educate myself. Everything was so confusing. I would end up in a psychiatric ward in shambles. During a depression I wouldn't even talk, shower or eat. During mania, I would scream, sing and shout through the hospital. It would take me weeks in a mental hospital to get stable. Not only was it hard on me, but my family, friends and hospital workers suffered with me.

Coming down from mania is very painful. It is hard on the brain and body. Finances and relationships suffered from me living untreated. If someone has a heart attack, they might take out books about heart disease from the library. They might talk to a nutritionist. They will have a close relationship with their doctor. Everyone in their life will probably be involved in some way. Their diet will likely change. They will try and learn what caused the heart attack. They will avoid things that can cause further damage to their heart. And if they don't? They can end up in the hospital, plain and simple.

The same goes for me. I keep a close relationship with my doctor. I research about bipolar disorder in the library and on the internet. Some articles could be good for me and others could have misleading information. One article can claim that diet and exercise will cure bipolar disorder. Another article might claim that cannabis oil will remove all bipolar symptoms. It is up to me to do my research. All of our brains are different. We all have different chemicals in our brains. My medication works for me. However, if my family member who has bipolar disorder takes my medication, they may not be treated properly. Our doctors and nurses have the proper education when it comes to medicine. Not everyone takes medication for bipolar disorder but for those who do, it is important to talk with the doctor before starting, stopping or changing medication.

Psychology is a science. Science can evolve and change over time. It is a good idea to stay current with bipolar disorder news and updates. Here are a few things that help me stay educated with bipolar disorder:

- Library books
- Bipolar disorder magazines
- Mental health websites
- Bipolar disorder support groups
- Psychiatrists
- Therapists
- Friends and family

It is never too early or late to get educated when it comes to bipolar disorder. Ask questions! Never feel ashamed for not knowing something. When I attend bipolar support groups, I see many people asking questions. We can feel safe in these places as well as with our medical team. Remember, knowledge is powerful when it comes to treating ourselves and leading our best life.

Medication

Depending on who you ask, there can be various ways to treat bipolar disorder. Some people believe that bipolar disorder can be treated holistically. Also, people may think that bipolar disorder can be treated through diet, exercise and supplements. I personally feel that medication can be a life saver. It is for me. However, I do believe in also having a healthy diet and living a healthy life to stay well. Whether a person has bipolar disorder or not, healthy food, exercise, sleep, sunlight and rest are all important.

As human beings, we have many basic needs. If you choose not to take medicine, you may choose to skip this chapter. However, if you currently take medication for bipolar disorder or are considering taking them, this chapter may be helpful for you. Make sure to consult your psychologist, psychiatrist and/or medical team before taking, changing or stopping medication.

I currently have been taking medication for bipolar disorder for over five years and I haven't seen the inside of a mental hospital since I got on the right medication. My medicinal regimen has literally saved my life. Does that mean that I do not work on myself and manage my illness? No. There is no magic pill. The same way a person with diabetes takes their medicine, watches what they eat and exercises, I too take good care of myself and take my medicine.

I live with my bipolar disorder but I also lead a successful and productive life. I owe this to taking my medicine daily. I have not missed a day in over five years. I know that the only reason for feeling as good as I do is because I do my part and stay on my medicine. The great part is, is that I only take two pills and one as needed. Also, I feel minimal side effects.

For one, I might feel slightly nauseous if I don't eat a big enough snack with my medicine. Secondly, I feel slightly tired. That's it. To me, if feels like a small price to pay to stay hospital free.

 Medicine is not always the easy part. Many men and women are concerned about weight gain with their medicine. Other side effects could be hair loss, insomnia and more. The important thing for me was to create a working relationship with my psychiatrist. I treat him as my partner and friend when it comes to my medicine. I let him know when I am worried that I could be feeling an odd side effect. I will ask him if it is possible to lower my dosages. I make sure to run everything by him and then he will help me with my medication.

 My first example is with my antipsychotic medication. It was set at eighty milligrams when I started seeing him. I would take my medicine every night but it would make me very nauseous. I also felt a lot of trouble getting up in the morning. With careful consideration, we lowered my antipsychotic medication to sixty milligrams. Now, it is perfect. I always want to lower my dosages just to have less chemicals in my body but I don't because I am stable. The chemicals in my brain are balanced with my medication. There are no visions, voices or grandiose plans. Mania is far in my past.

    Obtaining my antipsychotic was difficult in the beginning. I was going to a low budget outpatient facility. I had come out of a manic hospitalization for the third time. Once I got on my current antipsychotic, it was like night and day for me. It finally clicked that in order for me to stay well, medicine was part of my daily routine. A couple of years later, through education, I learned that I needed a mood stabilizer. My lows and highs in my mood were too drastic.

Amy Perez MS Psychology

    My rollercoaster ride of emotions ended with medical therapy. Also, I got diagnosed with anxiety so I take medicine for that as needed. I am no different than someone who takes cholesterol or diabetes medication. The key with medicine is to be honest with yourself and take medicine as prescribed and as needed. There is no shame in getting help and getting on the right medicine. As mentioned earlier about psychology being a science, that goes for medicine also, it's always changing. There are way more options for psychiatric drugs today than there was ten or even five years ago.

    The key is to balance the chemicals in our brain. I stay on a schedule with my medicine. I make sure to take it every night with food. I make sure not to drink a lot of alcohol before taking my medicine. If I have problems with my medicine, I make sure to speak with my psychiatrist right away. Here is an example of my path with medication to show that it can take a while to find a perfect fit:

2011 - Seroquel and Risperdal

2012 - Depakote and Abilify

2013 - Latuda

2015 - Latuda and Lamictal

As you can see, there was a path to reach the correct medicine for my brain. Medicine that works for me may not work for a close family member with bipolar disorder. Whether someone takes medicine or not, the goal is stability. I enjoy being stable. Even with medicine, the rest of the work is up to me. Being healthy takes time, self-love and patience. Medicine plays a key role for me. Taking my medicine allows me to thrive and work. Working is important to me. That topic will be covered next.

Amy Perez MS Psychology

Working

Working can be important to many of us with bipolar disorder. Some of us work out of necessity or pride or both. Working can distract the brain from problems. Working can provide us with exercise. Working can make us proud. However, bipolar disorder can be disabling. For some people, being on disability is a way to survive and thrive with bipolar disorder. That is okay. Whether a person is on disability or not, working can be therapeutic and fun.

For me personally, I enjoy working. Working is my escape. That doesn't always mean that I get paid for the work that I do. Many people have work to do around the house and yard. Many of us have children and pets. When I speak to other people with bipolar disorder, I realize that work is a trouble area. How can a mother with bipolar disorder work on laundry if she struggles to get out of bed? How can a man with bipolar disorder do yard work if he cannot cook and take a shower?

I have many solutions to these issues. My first solution is to make a list. List all of the things that need to get done in order of what is important for survival. Some days "surviving" is an uphill battle. Here is a list for today that is set up for me to survive and thrive:

-10:00 a.m. Brush teeth, have coffee and write

-11:30 a.m. Have breakfast, plan meals and chores for the day

-12:00 p.m. Practice self-care (wash face, get dressed etc.)

-1:00 p.m. Set a timer for thirty minutes and clean

-1:30 p.m. Have lunch, online shop for essentials like paper towel, cleaning supplies and dry goods. Also, make a grocery list for fresh items. In some areas, these items can be delivered to the home.

-2:00 p.m. Run errands

-3:00 p.m. Pick up my children from school

-4:00 p.m. Work (write, laundry, homework with the children, etc.)

-5:00 p.m. Start dinner and listen to music

-6:00 p.m. Eat dinner as a family

-6:30 p.m. Exercise either in the gym or outside

-8:30 p.m. Protein shake or snack

-9:30 p.m. Shower and self-care

-10:00 p.m. Relax, read, snack and take medicine

-11:00 p.m. Sleep

This is a typical busy work week. Some days there are doctor appointments. Those days I typically won't do any shopping and I will limit my time to get ready. I store easy meals in the pantry for the days that I don't have time to shop for dinner. My easy meals are also for the days that I am low on energy. I do all kinds of work throughout the day. There is writing work and housework. But the most important work is the work on myself. If I need to take a break than I do.

If all of the housework doesn't get done, that is okay. Even my friends and family who do not have bipolar disorder, never finish their housework. There will always be dishes, laundry and yard work. The work on ourselves always comes first. You cannot pour from an empty cup. We need to get clean, shower and practice self-care. Also, part of my self-care is doing work other than housework and writing. I have passions and dreams. There is no reason why someone with bipolar disorder can't work towards goals and dreams.

It just might need to fit our lives in a different way. Some of my college classes were online. Some of my shopping gets done online. Some days I don't get a lot of work done. Some days it is pizza for dinner because cooking is out of the question. That is okay. I have learned to not be hard on myself. Working means different things to different people. The most important work is the work on ourselves. It is important to do work that we are passionate about. Write, paint, draw or sing. This is the work that can get us out of depression. This work can bring us down from mania.

Amy Perez MS Psychology

Those of us with bipolar disorder are no different than anyone else. Whether we work full time, part time, are self-employed or receive disability. We all have work to do. Self-care is our most important job that we have. The work that we do on ourselves comes first. Not only can we survive with bipolar disorder, we can thrive and feel good. If you or someone you know is going through a hard time with bipolar disorder just know that you can get through it. Also, you are not alone. I am available through various social media accounts for questions for me.

10 Ways to Thrive With Bipolar Disorder

Amy Perez MS Psychology

Bipolar Disorder: Triggers Boundaries and Roadblocks (Preview)

Amy Perez MS Psychology

Amy Perez

MS

Psychology

Amy Perez MS Psychology

10 Ways to Thrive With Bipolar Disorder

Introduction

It's late, I've had a few drinks, there are a group of women flirting with my husband at a party and I skipped dinner after work. On top of that, it's close to the holidays and I miss my family. I walk outside of the party and sob uncontrollably into my hands. I'm so upset. So, I call my sister and spill out a whirlwind of emotion. My husband walks outside to find me. I blow up at him and scream in his face. I tell him that he doesn't love me. Then I storm down the street in anger. My husband, who is confused chases me down the street. Oh yeah, and I have bipolar disorder. So, what happened here?

For starters, I wasn't stable on my medication. But that wasn't the only thing at play here. There were some triggers going on:

- Jealousy
- Hunger
- Loneliness
- Sadness
- Holiday Stress
- Alcohol
- Large Crowd

These seven triggers were happening all at once. Back then, I didn't understand what was happening to my brain and within my body. I got off work and put myself into a situation that I wasn't ready for. I was already hungry. I was busy working to pay bills and I wanted to buy gifts for people. I was missing my family who lived far away. The icing on the cake was the women who were overly interested in my husband.

I was brought to tears with emotions such as anger, jealousy, stress and sadness. However, this was early after a bipolar disorder diagnosis. This was also before I started a Master's degree program in Psychology. Way before I finally got stable was a huge learning process. Unfortunately, just taking medicine was not enough. There was a process I needed to learn. I needed to learn what triggers were. Sometimes triggers are easy to spot. Others would show up when I least expect them.

    When we understand what triggers are and how to address them, we can create our life to deal with them. We can be prepared for triggers. We can practice self-care and educate ourselves as a form of protection to stay well. Sometimes, if a trigger is more severe, we will have to set boundaries. In an extreme case, we may even need to set a road block. In this book, we will break down triggers, boundaries and more. We will discuss self-care and why it is so important for someone with bipolar disorder. What is the point of all of this? The goal is to stay as well as possible. We want to live a stable life. Stability may look different for each person.

If you have bipolar disorder, you understand how important it is to stay stable. If you are a loved one of someone who has bipolar disorder, you also know how important it is for them to stay stable. I am both. I have bipolar disorder and I am a family member of people with bipolar disorder. I know what it's like to go through hospitalization in mania and depression. I have also watched loved ones go through it. My ultimate goal is to stay hospital free. I want this for myself as well as my loved ones. But beyond not being hospitalized, I want to be happy and I want to thrive in life. I want to recognize my triggers and limit or avoid them. Through recognizing triggers and setting boundaries, we can build a happy, stable life. We owe it to ourselves and loved ones. Let's get started.

Amy Perez MS Psychology

What is a Trigger?

The scary part is that a trigger could be anything. Each and every one of us are unique. We all have special experiences that make us who we are. We all have had good experiences and bad experiences. Everyone has things that make them happy as well as things that bring sadness. The confusing part is that these things can be different for all of us. Within an event, a wedding for instance, some people will feel happy, some sad and maybe some angry. Therefore, different events in a wedding can trigger different feelings for each person. Isn't the field of psychology fun? So, let's break down this wedding. At the wedding, the bride, groom and wedding guests all have a range of emotions. In addition to that, there are a lot of people who have a certain degree of mental health conditions. These include:

- Anxiety
- Addiction
- Depression
- Alcoholism
- Bipolar Disorder
- Schizoaffective Disorder

These are all clinical mental health disorders. They all require a visit with a doctor or therapist. Some require medicine for the person to stay stable. Some people may have two of these conditions. One person may have anxiety and also have an alcohol addiction. Another person can have bipolar disorder and also have a cigarette addiction. When we mix all of these people together with loud music, alcohol, dancing, food and of course the happy couple, there are bound to be some triggers. For the purpose of this book, we are going to focus on the person with bipolar disorder, me. I'm not the one getting married but I am still triggered by the event. Not only do I have bipolar disorder but I am the sister of the bride, the maid of honor, I am pregnant and I have guests staying at my place. On top of that, my father is staying with me because he is going through a divorce. Also, my husband just took an internship that cut his pay in half. Do you recognize any triggers? Let's list them out:

- Major life events
- Pregnancy
- Stress
- Emotions
- Loud music
- Loud people
- Pregnancy hormones
- Toxic people
- Alcohol
- Alcohol abuse
- Bright lights

- Financial stress

That is a large array of triggers. That is just going on at one event. Being able to recognize these triggers is what is so important. A trigger is anything that could cause an emotion that is good or bad. Even further, for someone with bipolar disorder, a trigger could cause an extreme low or high. A combination of triggers could send someone into a surge of mania or even deep depression. One trigger alone such as financial stress or loud music may not create too many symptoms for a stable person with bipolar disorder. Even all of the triggers at the wedding kept this person with bipolar disorder in check.

However, depending on stability, triggers such as these can prove that someone is overwhelmed with manic or depressive symptoms. During this time, I was practicing my steps in *10 Ways to Thrive with Bipolar Disorder* so I got through it with ease. I was able to get hit with multiple life events and I came out on top. However, a major trigger such as a death in the family could throw even the most stable person over the edge. Here is an example list of triggers that could set off manic or depressive symptoms in someone with bipolar disorder:

- Promotion
- Birth of a child
- Wedding
- Party
- Funeral
- Job loss
- Personal illness
- Illness in the family
- Death in the family
- Financial stress
- Season changes
- Emergency situations

- Loud music
- Bright lights
- Toxic people
- Dirty environments
- Sterile environments
- Unorganized environments
- Chaos
- Chaotic events
- Loud noises
- Sleep disruption
- Job stress
- Ending of a relationship
- Starting a new relationship
- Relationship stress
- Arguing
- Moving
- Starting a new career
- Caffeine

- Alcohol
- Drugs
- Poor diet
- Lack of exercise
- Poor life choices
- Heat
- Cold
- Discomfort
- Sharp objects
- Medicine/Pills

These are my top major triggers. Feel free to make a list of your own triggers. Your top trigger could be something completely different. It could be a person, place or thing. A song could trigger positive or negative emotions. There could be a person in your life who triggers positive or negative emotions or both. They may not even be aware that they are doing it. In an extreme case, a person could be doing it on purpose.

We will discuss how to deal with this through boundaries later in the book. In an extreme case, a roadblock may have to be set. Next, we will talk about how to handle triggers.

Made in the USA
Coppell, TX
06 April 2021